Kids in Print

Publishing a School Newspaper

Second Edition

by Mark Levin
Mind-Stretch Publishing

Thanks to the following for ideas, suggestions, and encouragement...

Bobbie Levin
Jane Miller
Claudia Sherry
Susan Eddy
Connie Fulkerson
Mignon Mandon
Kim Broshar

and a big thank you to the hundreds of NESPA members and the thousands of NESPA students who continue to be the inspirtation behind this book.

Graphic Design and Cover by Jo Northup, Jamlet Graphics • jamlet@bellsouth.net

Mind-Stretch Publishing
3124 Landrum Road
Columbus, NC 28722
www.mindstretch.com

ISBN-13: 978-0-9676409-2-1
ISBN-10: 0-9676409-2-X

4 5 6 7 8 9

Printed in the United States of America by
Morris Publishing, 3212 E. Highway 30, Kearney, NE 68847

Kids in Print

Publishing a School Newspaper
Second Edition

Contents

Why Publish a School Newspaper?

When I first started teaching language arts, I had difficulty finding the right balance of skills instruction and creative thinking instruction for a good writing program—one that might make kids *want* to write. While some activities and prompt sheets seemed appropriate to me, and a few even sounded interesting to students, one question was invariably posed first—how long does it have to be?

I had heard and read that students often write better for "real" audiences. But the only real audiences I could think of were families, or the travelers of school hallways who would occasionally glance at the papers adorning the walls. I had never thought of asking students to write the news. And it certainly never crossed my mind that kids could publish a newspaper on a regular basis—and have fun doing it.

Once I settled on the idea of a school newspaper, I received unanimous support. And what I learned is that kids *can* do it all. Publishing a newspaper fulfills many of the needs of a good writing program and offers other benefits as well.

★ Student and faculty readership provides a real audience on an ongoing basis.

★ Students are encouraged to write about things that are meaningful to them — to "write what they know."

★ The guidelines of journalistic style provide structure and discipline.

★ Deadlines hold students responsible and accountable.

★ Editing and rewriting (process-writing skills) are an important part of newspaper work.

★ Students have a voice. Responsible articles and editorials can impact their lives in school.

★ Newspapers provide a variety of real-world jobs and meet the needs of students of many abilities.

★ Great newspapers require great cooperative effort.

★ Students learn and apply real-life skills by publishing a paper: organizing, prioritizing, meeting deadlines, creative problem solving.

★ School newspapers are terrific public-relations pieces to give to visiting or recently-arrived parents, real estate offices, community libraries, and chambers of commerce.

Never have I seen students more excited about writing as when working on the newspaper. Suddenly students are begging for a whole page for their stories or realizing that an issue will require four additional pages if all the news is to be covered. And the excitement doesn't wane. We begin working on ideas for the next issue while waiting for the current one to arrive from the printer. Students take justifiable pride in their newspaper, and each issue provides an opportunity to brainstorm ideas for improvements in the next one. Publication of their articles validates students' work and their editorial opinions. When they are accountable to their reading public, students rise to the occasion magnificently!

There is no question that publishing a newspaper can be time-consuming. It also requires supreme organizational skills and flexibility. But it might just be the best thing you've ever accomplished in your classroom! You'll find just about everything you'll need to get you started in this book: a glossary; guidelines for teaching journalism skills, for organizing your staff, for choosing "beats;" tips for layout, design, and publication; and lots of reproducibles for organization and assessment.

Finally, you'll find a list of resources to help you as you look for ways to make your newspaper better. Publishing a newspaper can provide enormous motivation for kids to write. What are you waiting for?

This second edition of *Kids in Print—Publishing a School Newspaper* has been updated to bring you more common-sense information to help make your job easier. *Kids in Print* is the official how-to sourcebook for NESPA, an organization that helps elementary and middle schools publish school newspapers as a means of teaching meaningful writing skills. Hundreds of schools across the United States are members and the association has helped thousands of other schools get started.

And if you would like to know about or join **NESPA, the National Elementary Schools Press Association**, call (828) 274-0758 ext. 385 or fax (828) 277-8832 or check out the web site at: **www.nespa.org**. You can also write to me at the address below. I'll look forward to hearing from you and to reading your newspaper!

Mark Levin, Director
National Elementary Schools Press Association
Carolina Day School
1345 Hendersonville Road
Asheville, NC 28803

Organizing the Classroom

It's not hard to set up a professional newsroom. Most of the bare necessities are probably already in your classroom or close by. No doubt there will be other things going on in your classroom besides publication of the newspaper—this should not pose any problems. As your journalistic endeavors become more ambitious, your needs will grow. Consider posting a sign outside your door so people will know that your classroom is also the headquarters and production offices of the school newspaper. Your students will appreciate this little added touch of professionalism as well.

The Basics

Ruled paper

Dictionaries

Scissors, rulers, erasers

Glue

Fine-tipped markers

Books of clip art

File or pocket folders

Copier access

Clipboards

Sign-out and sign-in forms for reporters using the library or computer lab

Nice To Have

★ Thesaurus and Almanac

★ File cabinet or recycled copier paper boxes for file folders

★ Word processor and printer

★ Professional stylebook from Associated Press or similar source

★ Dedicated classroom space for your newsroom

★ Additional computers with page layout software

★ Extra floppy disks

★ Software with computer-generated clip art

★ Mailbox for each student

★ Camera and film

★ Manuals for layout and design

★ Drafting table, T Square, and triangles if paste-ups are done by hand

Wish List

★ Telephone

★ CD-Writer

★ Laser Printer

★ Digital camera

★ Scanner

★ Internet access, a home page for your newspaper, and e-mail to correspond with other schools

★ Networked computers so that articles and pages-in-progress can be saved to and retrieved from a school server.

★ Funding for professional printing

6

Organizing the Students

What They Need

All reporters need help getting organized. Ask that each student on the newspaper staff acquire a standard-sized three-ring notebook that will be dedicated to newspaper work. It is important that students be able to add dividers or designate different sections in some way. In addition, provide each student with a file or pocket folder that will remain in the classroom. If space allows, you may wish to have the notebooks stored in the classroom as well.

Current Issue

This is where notes and outlines are kept for stories that reporters are currently working on. Students may jot down their outlines, questions, headline and lead sentence ideas, and so on. Deadline schedules should also be kept here as well as style sheets and checklists. (see pages 17-22).

Future Issues

This is where reporters can keep notes on stories they've been assigned for future issues as well as schedules detailing their deadlines.

Story Ideas

Good reporters should always be on the lookout for new and exciting story possibilities. Be sure students have a place to jot their ideas down. Your community paper may be a good source of ideas—your school library should have a subscription.

Contacts

Whenever students meet someone with an interesting past, present, or future, that person's name, address, and phone number should go in this section. When it's time to write the story, reporters will know where to go for information. After the article is published, reporters may send a complimentary copy of the newspaper to that person. Of course, contacts for stories-in-progress could go here as well as in the section for current work.

Business Cards and Press Badges

Invite an interested student to design business cards and press badges for members of your staff or use the pattern on page 28. These can be laminated or inserted in badge holders and distributed to students to use as identification when they're out "getting a story." If possible, have students include pocket dividers in their notebooks for storing a supply of cards, a press badge, and other identifying credentials.

(Mind-Stretch Publishing offers "The Reporter's Notebook" with all of the above and much more ready for your students to use. See the resources on page 77 for ordering information.)

What They Do

It is highly desirable to turn over as much responsibility as possible to students (more on this later). Be sure students realize that they may have to give up some of their free time to help organize the paper. Choose editors who will be able to make decisions on their own, such as which articles go on which pages. Consider having two separate newspaper staffs, complete with two editors-in-chief *for each staff* (four in all). The two staffs may alternate—each publishing every other issue. This way, no one person gets all the blame or takes all the credit. It is often easier for students (and adults) to share responsibilities for decision-making.

Once you have done some work with students on journalism skills (see pages 35-57), it is time to assign staff positions. One effective and real-life method is to have students "apply" for the position they want by filling out job applications (see page 11) or by writing business letters to you with an attached resume. Brainstorm with students the different sections your newspaper will have. If possible, get several newspapers from other schools for your students to examine and critique. They'll find things they like and things they don't care for. Incorporate their ideas, and be flexible—some students may insist on a fashion column and others may prefer video games and movie reviews. NESPA, the National Elementary Schools Press Association (see the resources section of this book), can provide a few copies of sample newspapers.

When you have solidified the list of jobs that will be available, invite students to fill out applications or write letters to you using proper business format. In the letters they should give you their first and second choices of staff positions and tell why they would perform those jobs well. If you wish, you may ask students to include writing samples, or art samples if applying for a job as an editorial cartoonist. When you have the applications, letters, and writing samples, you can more easily set up your staff. Of course, you will want to give some priority to students who have worked on the newspaper in the past. In addition, you will want to try to set up mentoring relationships between experienced students and "cub" reporters.

Of course, be prepared for some hurt feelings when each student doesn't get the job of his or her first choice. Remind the class that publishing a newspaper is a team effort and everyone's job is important.

Here are some jobs you might be filling. Keep in mind that no one newspaper will have all of these positions on staff, and you may need positions that do not appear on this list. You may wish to have students work in the same staff positions on at least two consecutive issues—or all year. This way they can build on experience from the first issue to the second and throughout the year. You might want to name two or three students to certain positions just to give more students those responsibilities. Everyone likes to have a job.

Editor in Chief

This student (or students) oversees the entire newspaper. Their job is to see that all deadlines are met and that the paper goes to press on time. They also might make editorial decisions when articles need to be shortened or cut altogether.

Assistant Editor

If you have only one editor in chief, you may wish to have a younger student act as assistant. This provides great on-the-job training for future editors in chief.

Editorial Board

This can actually be a group of students, possibly current or former section editors. This board can make content decisions as a group, such as when to take out an article so that it doesn't offend or embarrass someone. Professional newspapers offend and embarrass people all the time—but doing so in elementary and middle schools can lead to trouble in a hurry.

News Editor

This is the student in charge of the "hard" news section, as opposed to features. This may include both school and community news, such as class elections or a community zoning issue. This student will assign articles to news reporters and establish deadlines for those articles. He or she may also do some editing on those articles.

Feature Editor

This student is in charge of the "soft" news section. This may include both school and appropriate community news, such as social events and interviews. This student will assign articles to feature reporters and establish deadlines for those articles. He or she may also do some editing of those articles.

Sports Editor

This student or students (you may with to have a girl and a boy if there is a great deal to cover) will write and edit sports news. There is rarely a need for more than two students on the sports staff. If your school is large, an additional reporter or two may work on this section.

Tracking Manager

This student keeps track of what was covered in each issue so that the same teacher or student isn't written about three times during the year while someone else is never mentioned. This student would have a writing job as well.

Business Manager

This student is in charge of the day-to-day management of any funds received or spent. He or she should send thank-you notes for any donations received. An added bonus would be for a business manager to provide "profit & loss" statements on a regular basis.

Circulation Manager

This student keeps track of subscriptions and sees that papers are distributed when they arrive from the printer or come off the school copier. This includes deliveries to classrooms as well as the mailing of paid subscriptions, if any. The circulation manager should make sure all the teachers and administrators get copies—and don't forget to leave several copies in the main office.

Art Director

This may be a job for one or two students who are responsible for choosing clip art, drawing original art (where needed), and overseeing the look of the paper. They might help other students with layout design help.

Book, TV, Movie, CD, Video Game, or Restaurant Reviewers

One or two students may review a variety of media or a local restaurant for each issue of the newspaper. Remind them that they are writing an opinion piece and should follow the rules for editorial writing on page 44.

Horoscope

One student may enjoy creating a horoscope column for each issue. Old horoscope columns for reference may prove useful. Horoscopes are fun to write and are usually popular sections in the papers that choose to include them.

Advertising Manager

This is the student who receives classified ads, edits them for content, and organizes them for the newspaper. If your newspaper accepts display ads, the advertising manager may need a staff as well.

Roving Reporter

This student chooses an interesting, relevant question on which there may be many opinions and obtains those opinions from as many people as possible for his or her column.

Reporters

These students, while not in "management" positions, are assigned to write for certain sections (beats) of the newspaper. On a small paper, everyone will probably need to be a reporter. It should be emphasized that there can't be a paper without the reporters-they are the backbone of every newspaper.

Photographers

While individual reporters can be encouraged to take their own photos, it is doubtful you'll want every reporter using the newspaper's camera. It's best to train a photography corps of about three or four students and let them take the majority of the photos. With a little experience, these students can produce some really good results.

Job Application

Name _____
Address _____
_____
Phone _____ **Grade** _____
Homeroom Teacher _____ **Room** _____

Why do you want to be on the newspaper staff? _____

_____

_____

What staff position would you like? 1st Choice _____

2nd Choice _____ 3rd Choice _____

Why would you like these jobs? _____

_____

_____

Have you worked on a newspaper before? _____

What job did you have? _____

I understand that if I am offered a job on the newspaper, I am taking on extra responsibilities and that my regular class work must still be handed in on time.
Student's Signature _____ **Date** _____

How They Do It

The section of this book entitled "Teaching Journalism Skills" (see pages 35-57) provides plenty of ideas for teaching writing skills to your staff. But writing is only the beginning. Here are some teacher-tested tips for ensuring that all aspects of the publication process are covered.

At the beginning of the year, teach students the basics of page layout. If you are not familiar with the software you will be using, enlist the aid of your technology or computer instructor. Some programs that might come pre-installed on your computer might offer limited design options, but these are often powerful enough for most elementary and middle school newspaper needs. If you wish to move up to more professional features, programs like Microsoft's Publisher and Adobe's PageMaker or InDesign will handle most anything your kids will ever need. Of course, with any program, become familiar with it before attempting to teach it to your students.

If they do not already know these skills, students will need to learn how to open a new document, save the document, insert text blocks or boxes, insert photos and graphics, wrap text, create columns, and change fonts and point sizes for starters. Time spent early in the year learning the basics makes things run more smoothly down the line.

Keep in mind that this generation of students has practically grown up using computers. What seems daunting to you may literally be child's play for them. Invite students who have mastered the basics to help mentor others. There is a good chance a student or two will enter your classroom in the fall already accomplished in desktop publishing. Put them to work right away. See pages 58-60 for more on layout and design.

After students have completed the "near-to-final" page layouts, make photocopies for each staff member and sit down with the group for a quiet read-through. All students then become editors, making changes with appropriate editorial symbols (see page 57). Work one page at a time (and suggest they tackle the page one paragraph at a time) rather than giving students the entire page at once. Class members then go through each page line by line, paragraph by paragraph, giving their thoughts on changes. After this final round of editing takes place (this can take a couple of days), reporters or editors may make the necessary changes and print the final paste-up. Don't rush this step!

You may wish to have two students responsible for each page of the newspaper—from its inception to final camera-ready layout. Those two students might write the articles and do initial editing or just layout the page with articles written by other staff members and add the graphics. After the class editing session, each pair goes back and makes any needed changes to their page. On the final deadline, students present the editor-in-chief with camera-ready paste-ups, which then go either to the printer or the copy machine.

On the pages that follow are several forms that may be useful in organizing your staff. Adapt these to fit your needs whenever necessary.

The **Work Progress Schedule** is used to set due dates for each step of the publication. Your schedule will vary depending on factors such as whether work is done at home, at school, by a newspaper club, or as a class project. A calendar would work just as well. Be sure to post this schedule and duplicate a copy for each student.

The **Reporter Assignment Form** is used to assign topics to students for a particular issue. Sometimes students choose their assignments, and at other times, articles arc assigned. This form is kept in the student's personal newspaper file folder or notebook. You or the editor-in-chief may wish to retain copies as well.

The **Details Checklist** is used by students to help get the facts when researching, interviewing for, and writing their articles.

A **Revision Checklist** is used by peer-editors, staff editors, or teachers when helping students edit their work. You will need at least two per article during the writing process.

The **Student Work Progress Record** is used by students to keep track of their work-in-progress. You may wish to three-hole punch these for students to keep in their binders. Have editor(s) take responsibility for signing off when assignments are complete. This form may also be used to determine a final writing grade for each student for each issue.

The **Class List of Reporting Assignments** is used to keep track of reporting assignments for the entire class. You and the editor(s) should have copies, and you may wish to post one as well.

The **Page Layout Assignment Form** is used when assigning a student or team of students complete responsibility for the writing or layout of one camera-ready page.

The **Writing Style Sheet** is used to help strive for consistency in the formatting of the newspaper. The information on the style sheet included with *Kids in Print* is based on the one used by the staff of *Carolina Kids' News*. You'll need to adapt your own to your situation. This style sheet was prepared to help *Carolina Kids' News* reporters work in pairs to produce a camera-ready page. It helps them be consistent in completing their entirely student-produced newspaper.

The **Article Tracking Form** is used by the tracking manager to keep track of who wrote about what in which issue. This helps achieve balanced coverage by preventing too much press about one individual.

Teacher Grading Work Sheets are used to keep track of student progress and grades each step of the way. The first worksheet has suggested grading sections included; the second is blank so that you may customize your own form.

The **To Do List** can be used by students to keep track of assignments or things to do and as a reporter's notepad if cut and mounted on cardboard or clipboard. You might find a bunch of other uses for them as well.

Press Badges may be personalized and cut to fit standard business-card-sized plastic badge holders found at office supply stores. Use the top line for the name of each student and the block for the name of the newspaper or school. These cards should also line up perfectly with the many varieties of preprinted and perforated card stock available from specialty paper suppliers (see page 80) or from larger office supply stores. Many desktop publishing programs include templates built-in for making professional-looking business cards in a snap. Or, check out the ready-to-go templates at: www.avery.com.

Work Progress Schedule

Issue Date _____ **Publication Date** _____

To Press Date (one week prior to "publication" date) _____

Polish (Final Proofing) Date (two days prior to "to press" date) _____

Typesetting Date (five days prior to "polish" date) _____

Final Copy Date (two days prior to "typesetting" date) _____

Edited Copy Date (five days prior to "final copy" date) _____

Rough Draft Date (seven days prior to "edited copy" date) _____

Work Days

Two days prior to and/or including the "rough draft" date _____

One day prior to the "edited copy" date _____

One day prior to the "final copy" date _____

A Comment — *Of course, this schedule is only a suggested schedule for staffs that meet regularly such as language arts or journalism classes. If your newspaper is published by a club or after-school program, your schedule will need to be adjusted to fit the time you have. Newspaper work should be fun. Do what you can when you can.*

Notes _____

_____

_____

_____

Reporter Assignment Form

Issue Date _____ **Reporter** _____

Article assigned _____

Basic "angle" for article_____

_____

Approximate length of article _____

Contact _____ Phone_____

Additional Contact _____ Phone_____

_____ **Rough draft due** _____

_____ **Edited copy due** _____

_____ **Final copy** _____

Special Notes_____

_____

_____

_____

_____

_____

Article assigned by _____ **Date Assigned** _____

Name _____

Details Checklist

Article _____ **Issue Date** _____

Who? _____

Details _____

_____

_____

_____

What? _____

Details _____

_____

_____

_____

Where? _____

Details _____

_____

_____

_____

When? _____

Details _____

_____

_____

_____

Why and/or how? _____

Details _____

_____

_____

_____

Notes _____

_____

_____

Revision Checklist

Name _____

Article _____ Issue Date _____

- ❏ Does the article have a catchy headline? What is is? _____

  _____

  _____

- ❏ Does the headline relate well to the article?

- ❏ Does the first sentence or lead catch the reader's attention?

- ❏ Does the first sentence or lead set the tone for the article that follows?

- ❏ Does the entire article make sense?

- ❏ Does the article follow an orderly sequence?

- ❏ Are all sentences complete?

- ❏ Do individual sentences make sense?

- ❏ Does the article include good descriptions?

- ❏ Does the article answer the following questions?

  - ❏ Who?
  - ❏ What?
  - ❏ Where?
  - ❏ When?
  - ❏ Why?

- ❏ Does the article have a strong conclusion?

Notes _____

_____

_____

_____

_____

Article read and edited by _____
Date_____

 18

Name _____

Student Work Progress Record

Issue Date _____ **Publication Date** _____ **To Press Date** _____

Your Assignment
List three possible ideas or angles for your article.

1. _____

2. _____

3. _____

*I will interview*_____ *on (date)*_____

Work Record

(to be initialed by advisor or editor)

Rough draft completed on time_____

First Revision_____

Second Revision_____

Final copy received on time_____

Due Dates

Rough Draft_____

Edited Copy_____

Final Copy_____

Final Copy

(to be checked by advisor or editor)

❏ has headline and byline

❏ is double-spaced

❏ is neatly written or typed

❏ uses correct spelling

❏ uses correct punctuation

❏ uses complete sentences

❏ has been checked for accuracy

Class List of Reporting Assignments

Issue Date _____

Name _____

Assignment _____

_____

Name _____

Assignment _____

_____

Name _____

Assignment _____

_____

Name _____

Assignment _____

_____

Name _____

Assignment _____

_____

Name _____

Assignment _____

_____

Page Layout Assignment Form

Issue Date _____

Page # _____ Editor assigned to this page _____

Section name for this page _____

Page assigned to (names) _____

Deadline for editing and final approval _____ Deadline for final layout _____

Articles to be included on this page:

Subject	Reporter

1. _____
2. _____
3. _____
4. _____

Special notice or feature to be included on this page: _____

Special layout and design notes: _____

_____

_____

_____

Additional notes: _____

_____

_____

_____

Be sure to include at least one graphic. Photographs are preferred.

Sample Style Sheet

Newspapers need to develop and stick with a style sheet to help bring a unified look to their newspaper. The items here are just suggestions. Once you've defined the "style" of your newspaper—have plenty of copies around the newsroom and insist that your students use them.

1. Center headline in boldface type using Comic Sans MS.

2. Use 14, 16, or 18 point type for the headline.

3. Center byline under headline (byline is not boldface) using this format: by Your Name (by is lowercase).

4. Byline should be 12 point Comic Sans MS.

5. Skip two lines before text of article.

6. Indent the beginning of each paragraph with one tab space.

7. Articles should be typed in 12 point Times New Roman font.

8. Articles should be typeset flush left, ragged right. Do *not* justify the right margin.

9. Use a teacher's first and last name the first time it is mentioned in your article. Then, use Mr., Mrs., or Ms.

10. Make sure there are no spaces between words and the punctuation marks that immediately follow.

11. Skip just *one* space between sentences.

12. Spell out numbers ten and smaller— use numerals for 11 and greater. However, never start a sentence with a numeral.

13. Use lowercase when referring to classes. For example, fifth grade, kindergarten.

14. Use italics when referring to books, movies, magazines, plays, etc. Do not underline.

15. All photos should have a caption. Captions should be in Times New Roman font, 10 point size, and italicized.

16. Always use the computer's spellchecker, but remember it will miss plenty of mistakes.

17. Save, save, save, and save again. You should save to a floppy as well as the school's server.

18. If your work is submitted on disk or electronically, you still need to submit a hard copy.

Article Tracking Form

Student	Article/Issue	Article/Issue	Article/Issue	Article/Issue	Article/Issue	Article/Issue	Article/Issue	Article/Issue

Teacher Grading Work Sheet

Student	Interview Preparation	Rough Draft	Edited Copy	Final Copy	Final Grade

Teacher Grading Work Sheet

Student					

Name _____

To Do List

✔ *When completed*   *Priority 1-2-3*

❏ _____ ❏
❏ _____ ❏
❏ _____ ❏
❏ _____ ❏
❏ _____ ❏
❏ _____ ❏
❏ _____ ❏
❏ _____ ❏
❏ _____ ❏
❏ _____ ❏
❏ _____ ❏
❏ _____ ❏
❏ _____ ❏
❏ _____ ❏
❏ _____ ❏
❏ _____ ❏
❏ _____ ❏
❏ _____ ❏
❏ _____ ❏
❏ _____ ❏
❏ _____ ❏
❏ _____ ❏
❏ _____ ❏

Name _____

To Do List

✔ *When completed*   *Priority 1-2-3*

❏ _____ ❏
❏ _____ ❏
❏ _____ ❏
❏ _____ ❏
❏ _____ ❏
❏ _____ ❏
❏ _____ ❏
❏ _____ ❏
❏ _____ ❏
❏ _____ ❏
❏ _____ ❏
❏ _____ ❏
❏ _____ ❏
❏ _____ ❏
❏ _____ ❏
❏ _____ ❏
❏ _____ ❏
❏ _____ ❏
❏ _____ ❏
❏ _____ ❏
❏ _____ ❏
❏ _____ ❏
❏ _____ ❏

Earning Your Credentials

Student staff members should be challenged to gain a working knowledge of journalism. You, as their teacher, can develop a list of skills students should master before being presented with his or her credentials. Credentials could include a certificate, a press badge, or even business cards.

Develop your own list of skills, but some possibilities include...

Do you know how to?

❏ Type (using a word processor) at a speed of _____ words per minute.

❏ Change fonts, point sizes, use italics, bold, center text, etc.

❏ Save your work to a disk and to the server or harddrive.

❏ Import a photograph or graphic.

❏ Wrap text around a photograph or graphic.

❏ Add captions to graphics.

❏ Create a layout using text blocks.

Students should also...

❏ Know basic journalism vocabulary.

❏ Be able to write interesting interview questions.

❏ Understand the 5 Ws.

❏ Understand interviewing etiquette.

Press Badges

Press ★ STAFF

Press ★ STAFF

Press ★ STAFF

Press ★ STAFF

Press ★ STAFF

Press ★ STAFF

Press ★ STAFF

Press ★ STAFF

 28

Organizing the Newspaper

Start with the Basics

If your school has not previously published a newspaper and you are starting from scratch, your newspaper will need a name. You may wish to handle this as a school-wide contest or simply take ideas from your staff and have them vote.

Once a name is selected, invite students to design the nameplate (the "logo" or look of the paper's name that stays the same from issue to issue). Students can use the computer and a desktop publishing program to help in their design. You might also post this nameplate design on a sign outside your classroom. Remind students that the design must reproduce well—intricate details are inappropriate. Designs should be rendered in black on white.

Once you have assigned staff positions, you will want to make up a production schedule for each issue. Some newspaper advisors are able to have all the writing done in school or after school, depending on when the staff meets. Others must assign some of the work as homework. Set realistic deadlines for article ideas, rough drafts, finished articles, page layouts, and camera ready-paste-ups. Be sure each student has a copy of the schedule, which should be posted in your classroom as well.

Set Realistic Goals

Keep in mind that in order for the newspaper to be a true learning experience, the students need to do the work. Aim high. Be absolutely insistent on certain standards, such as being sure that every name that appears in the paper is spelled correctly. Then relax and let the kids take over. If your editorial review processes are thorough and your editors are on the job, the result will be a paper you can all be proud of. You will need to provide plenty of guidance and constant reminders. A school newspaper is *never* about making the advisor look good. It is *always* about giving kids an opportunity to express themselves in writing in a public forum in a format that is professional and realistic.

Try not to take on more than you can handle. While the newspaper process can be a wonderful way to teach language arts, it is not meant to be so overwhelming that the whole experience becomes an ordeal. If that happens, neither you nor the students are going to have any fun. If this is your first year as the advisor, a realistic number of issues to publish would probably be one or two. Yes, the issues will be big and some of the news will be a bit stale. But you and your staff will have the luxury of time in which to create great graphics, cartoons, and puzzles; write thoughtful and incisive editorials; and in general produce a masterpiece. And you will *all* be learning.

Brainstorm Article Ideas

Students will have plenty of ideas for regular columns and features. You may wish to assign a student (or a team) to the same topic for every issue, or you may prefer to rotate students on a regular basis.

There is no reason why features must remain identical from issue to issue. For students to have ownership of their paper, they should make decisions concerning what works and what does not. For example, if an advice column draws letters that are obviously pranks, students may choose to discontinue the feature. On the other hand, answering prank letters in a humorous vein might make an interesting column! Some possible topics follow:

Class News

You may wish to have a student from each class or grade level send their news to your paper. You can alternatively assign staff members to cover particular classes or grade levels.

Editorials

Students may choose to write on kid-oriented topics or on more global issues.

A Word From the Principal

Invite the principal or another administrator to contribute a column about school happenings.

People Behind the Scenes

Students may enjoy writing features on your school's unsung heroes, such as administrative assistants, maintenance staff, custodians, administrators, guidance counselors, nurses, lunchroom workers, volunteers, coaches, assistant teachers, substitutes, and student teachers.

School Clubs

If there is a club program in your school, consider covering special club events or activities in your newspaper.

Calendar of Events

Depending on the number of issues you publish each year, you may wish to include a monthly or quarterly calendar of school-wide events. Although these schedules often change at the last minute, most sports events and things involving use of the auditorium or all-purpose room remain constant.

Sports

In addition to coverage of interscholastic competitions, sports news might include notes from the physical education teachers on what is happening in various classes, information on specific students and their athletic accomplishments, and coverage of league sports in the community. Sports articles could also feature non-traditional or non-school sports such as mountain biking, fencing, and equestrian activities.

30

Subject News

This would include news on special events in particular subject areas that may not be included in class news, such as a science fair or international festival that everyone will be invited to attend.

Restaurant/Book/Movie/CD/Software Reviews

Movies reviewed should probably be "G" rated so that all readers of your paper can attend. If CDs are reviewed, insist on previewing the lyrics. Some of this work will require parental support; however, these reviews are always an interesting and popular feature.

Horoscopes

Students may wish to create exotic aliases for horoscope columns. Provide reference information for signs of the zodiac.

Interviews

Subjects can be teachers, administrators, students, or community members. Be sure to include photos and set exact guidelines for procedure and protocol before sending students out for interviews (see pages 51-54). Some teachers may be willing to provide baby or elementary-school pictures to accompany their interviews.

Kids in the News

If there are students involved in interesting activities outside of school or who have accomplished something out-of-the-ordinary, you may wish to have students write about their activities for the newspaper.

Advice Column

Invite letters from readers asking for advice on certain issues. Letters may be written anonymously, if you prefer. Answers can come from students, teachers, or school counselors. Please be cautioned that students might not give appropriate advice, either because they don't have the life experiences necessary or because they just wish to be silly or "mean." Advisors must read and approve all answers before publishing.

Hobby Column

Invite experts to write about how to get started in a new hobby. Old favorites might include sports-card collecting, model building, and stamp collecting. New ideas could include collecting autographs, postcards, or arrowheads; origami; and kite building.

School Counselor Speaks!

Invite your school counselor to provide a column for each issue on making friends, being new, doing your best, and so on.

Study Skills How-to

Advice from kids and teachers on making the most of your time. Topics might include study habits, how to scan a book, how to make an outline, and how to prioritize.

What's New in the School Library

Your librarian may agree to supply a column for each issue listing new acquisitions. If possible, have students on your staff read and review some or all of the new books.

Places to Visit in the Community

What is there to see and do in your town? Provide descriptions of places that might be linked to courses of study in your school or that are just-for-fun family places. Include prices, telephone numbers, and other important information.

Consumer Testing

Invite reporters to test and compare things such as bubble gum, sneakers, video games, or any other category or product that students express interest in. Be sure to establish procedures for product testing so that tests are consistent and results are fair.

Games and Puzzles

Consider including crosswords, word searches, and similar activities in each issue. Activities may be theme related. There is excellent software available to help students design this type of thing (see page 80).

Did You Know?

These are short bits that include interesting, little-known facts about the school, community, or familiar people.

Guest Forum

Consider soliciting features, editorials, or inspirational pieces from friends, parents, and supporters of your school. Perhaps local writers or journalists would be willing to send short articles.

Classifieds

This section includes ads contributed by people in the school who have things to sell, give away, or trade. There is no charge for this advertising.

Jokes

There is never a shortage of material for this column. Invite students to write original jokes as well as recycling old ones.

A Day in the Life of...

Reporters may enjoy spending a day with a teacher, administrator, staff member, or another student and writing an article about the experience.

Guess Who?

This is a contest with clues to the identity of a student, teacher, or other staff member. Try to offer a prize, such as a credit at the school store or a free ice cream in the lunchroom, to the first successful respondent. Or, all correct entries get entered into a drawing with one or two winners selected at random.

Roving Reporter

In this section a reporter asks one opinion question of a number of people from all areas of the school. This question should be one of general interest.

Editorial Cartoons

Do you have a good classroom artist? Put his/her creative talents to good use. Editorial cartoons aren't easy to conceive, and even harder to convey to readers. Take some time to explain the concept of editorial cartooning. Find some examples to show, and then let kids try their hand. It's easier for kids to come up with an idea if they're drawing a cartoon based on something that is happening at school or should be happening at school. Some examples might include: soda machines in the lunchroom, less homework, letting younger students play interscholastic sports.

by Mary Robinson

Institute an Awards Program

One way to motivate students to do quality work is to create a program that rewards both excellence and effort. Do not limit the number of awards that can be earned in each category. Students might even win two or three awards for one article.

You can print terrific-looking certificates on a laser or ink jet printer by using high quality paper preprinted with an embellished border. This type of paper can be found at large office-supply stores or print shops or ordered from paper-supply companies (see page 80). Or you can use plain paper and create certificates with borders by using programs such as Print Shop Deluxe. Here are some awards you might consider.

Excellence in News Writing

This is given for a hard news story that answers the five Ws and makes a great, gripping read.

Excellence in Feature Writing

This is the same as above, but is given for features—stories more about the "human" side of the news that are lighter in content and structure.

Excellence in Editorial Writing

Given for well-written editorials that clearly define issues and make good cases for agreement or disagreement.

Excellence in Headline Writing

Given for exceptional headline writing— a skill all its own.

Excellence in Lead Writing

Given for compelling first sentences or paragraphs that grab the attention of the reader.

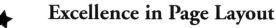

Excellence in Page Layout

Given for aesthetics of how a page looks including balance of copy to white space and use of graphics. This award should only be given if your students do the actual layout.

Excellence in Article Concept

Sometimes a student has a tremendous idea, works extremely hard, but still the article falls a little short. This award recognizes that effort.

Excellence in Photography

Given for exceptional, eye-catching photography.

The Publisher's Prize

Given for extraordinary effort and dedication to the newspaper publishing experience. This special award is only given when it is clearly deserved, and not necessarily after every issue.

Jargon

Students will enjoy learning the jargon of the newspaper industry. Many of the terms found in the following glossary are important for your staff to learn. Make copies of the glossary to distribute to everyone working on the newspaper and encourage students to use appropriate terminology as often as possible.

angle

the focus of a story; the approach a reporter takes to giving the facts.

beat

the area of news a reporter covers.

budget

planned allotment of funds depending on how much money a newspaper spends and receives in the course of publishing the paper.

byline

the line identifying the writer of a newspaper article.

caption

(also cutline)—an explanation of a photo, drawing, or graph.

classified ads

small ads for goods or services normally listed by category.

column

a regular series of articles or features in a newspaper. Also, the vertical sections of printed newspaper matter.

columnist

a staff writer who does a regular feature or article.

copy

text of an article.

correspondent

someone who contributes regularly to a newspaper, often from outside the immediate area.

dateline

the line at the beginning of a story naming the city or place of origin and often including the date.

departments

regular areas of news covered in a newspaper.

desktop publishing

a method of publishing that utilizes computers and special software that enable the staff to assemble the elements of a newspaper on-screen, without having to do mechanical paste-ups.

display ad

an ad that contains graphics as well as copy.

edit

to make changes to an article for a variety of reasons: clarity, length, mechanics, and so on.

editor

person who manages the various sections of the newspaper. The person may also make editorial decisions regarding content, length, or mechanics. The **editor-in-chief** manages the entire newspaper.

editorial

an article on a timely issue that expresses the opinion of the writer.

evergreen story

a story, usually a feature, that can be used at any time because it's not tied into a news angle.

exclusive

an article based on information granted to one particular news reporter or newspaper.

features

stories about people and their lives rather than news-related facts. Sometimes called soft news.

font

style of type used in a publication.

graphics

art, photography, charts, graphs, and other design features in a publication.

halftone

technique of representing photographs by a series of dots of various shades for reproduction in a publication.

hard news

straight news, including all the facts.

headline

title of a news article.

interview

a meeting in person, by phone, or by email in which a reporter asks questions in order to get information for a story.

 36

inverted pyramid style

the practice of placing the most important news information at the beginning of an article and proceeding through remaining details in order of importance. Most hard news is written in this style, which allows the reader to scan headlines and proceed to read as much information as is interesting or necessary.

layout

the overall design of a publication, including placement of headlines, articles, and graphics.

lead paragraph or sentence

the first sentence or paragraph in an article. It sets the tone for the article and hopefully entices the audience to read on.

libel

the act of damaging someone's reputation by what has been printed or written.

masthead

title of the newspaper and other important facts.

media

all forms of getting information to the public, including print, broadcast, and online.

morgue

where all back issues of newspapers are kept for reference.

name plate

the formatting of the name of the newspaper on the front page.

news tip

information a reporter receives that helps in the finding or writing of a news story.

obituary

a notice about a person's death.

paste-up

the final camera-ready layout of the newspaper with everything pasted, waxed, or taped in place. Most schools use desktop publishing software in which everything is "pasted up" electronically.

point

the measurement system that determines the size of type or font. The larger the number, the larger the letters. One point equals 1/72 of an inch, so 36 point type is 1/2 inches in height.

printer

the people who print the newspaper.

publisher

often the owner of the newspaper, who usually has overall responsibility for finances and editorial decisions. In schools this would probably be the teacher or the advisor. Occasionally the principal or even the school serves as publisher.

putting the paper to bed

when the paste-up (either manual or electronic) is complete and the paper is ready for printing.

retraction

a notice in a newspaper that cites an error the paper has made and is now correcting or retracting.

scoop

getting a breaking news item into print before your competitors do.

sidebar

a special design feature in a news or feature story that includes extra information, such as "where to write for more information," or "the location of a restaurant" a reporter might have reviewed and the hours of operation.

soft news

feature stories.

stringer

someone not necessarily employed by a newspaper but who sends in articles from time to time.

syndicated

when a reporter sells or submits an article for publication in many newspapers through a syndicate. The National Elementary Schools Press Association (see page 75) operates an online syndicate for student writing.

volume number, issue number

volume number refers to the number of years a paper has been published; issue number refers to the sequence of publications in the current year. For example, a newspaper publishing its second issue of the year in its third year of publication would use this notation: Volume 3, Number 2.

Journalistic Style

Most of the writing that students do for your newspaper will fall into one of two categories—the journalistic style or the editorial style. Younger students (and many adults) tend to confuse the two. So one of your many roles as an advisor should be to help students understand the important differences between these styles.

Students use the journalistic style when reporting hard news. This style consistently utilizes at least four of the five Ws—who, what, when, where, why or how—in the lead paragraph. It is important for students to understand that their stated opinions are not appropriate in this type of writing. Writing hard news is writing to inform, *not* writing to persuade. Facts must be stated clearly and without bias, allowing readers to form their own opinions.

Teaching Ideas ★ Teaching Ideas Teaching Ideas

Discuss the five Ws (who, what, when, where, why or how) by supplying students with short news articles from your city or community newspaper. Challenge pairs of students to locate each W and mark it in the way you designate, such as by color coding. Tally the results to see which Ws appear most often. Try to offer selections that present the five Ws in a variety of ways.

Have students write short news articles about a recent event at school. Invite volunteers to read their stories aloud and have students note the Ws that are covered. If an important W is not included, ask students to add a sentence that will rectify the omission. There will be times when one of the five Ws may be irrelevant, unnecessary, or unobtainable—help students learn to discriminate.

Practice news writing by taking your entire class to observe a school event, such as an assembly program. Each student is to work independently and should be prepared to take notes and conduct interviews, if appropriate. Return to your classroom and invite students to write articles on what they've just seen. This is a good time to discuss angles—the focus and approach of a news story. Volunteers may read their articles and comparative discussions should follow. If you have time, you may wish to have students input their articles on word processors and print them out. Assign each student a number with which to identify their articles—no names should appear. Duplicate as many complete sets of articles as there are students on the staff. Invite each student to read the complete set of articles and choose a favorite for discussion. You may reveal the identity of the student whose work is chosen as the favorite most often, if you wish.

Teach the concept of the inverted pyramid style of writing, using the reproducibles on pages 42-43. The most important news facts, including the five Ws, come first—at the broad top of the inverted pyramid. The reporter must prioritize facts and information in order to correctly utilize the inverted pyramid, saving the least important (but still interesting) information for the bottom. Explain that editors must often cut articles in order to fit them into the allotted space. It's easier and faster to cut from the end of an article than to go through and edit for importance. The inverted pyramid approach also allows readers to scan the paper for items of interest and become informed without reading beyond the first couple of paragraphs. This is particularly important for large city dailies, whose readers rarely have the time or interest to read every article from start to finish.

Use photos cut from magazines or newspapers to practice writing attention-grabbing headlines and lead sentences. Be sure to remove any captions. Explain that readers often scan a newspaper looking for headlines, subheads, and lead sentences that catch their interest. Lead sentences may either be written as straight factual statements incorporating a number of the five Ws, or students may use an intriguing statement or question to draw readers into their articles. You may wish to have students try one of each. For example, "The school cafeteria, which has tried for years to get students to eat vegetables, is proposing a new nutrition-based plan to get students to eat healthy." Or, "On Wednesday afternoon in the cafeteria at Old Turnpike Middle School, a hungry group of twelve-year-olds were invited to take part in a strange new eating adventure." Encourage students to share their work. Invite constructive comments from the class.

Find example of news stories that include quotes from pertinent people. Make overhead transparencies of the articles. Discuss with students why a quote might have been used rather than a paraphrase. Help students understand how a variety of sentence approaches adds interest and texture to their writing. Encourage students to practice writing news stories that alternate between facts and quotes.

A Few Ways to Say "Said"

Added	★	Chanted	★	Confirmed
Agreed		Cheered		Cried
Asked	★	Chided	★	Decided
Babbled		Claimed		Declared
Begged	★	Comforted	★	Demanded
Bragged		Commented		Denied
Cackled	★	Concluded	★	Described
Challenged		Confided		Echoed

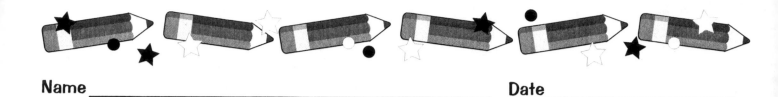

Inverted Pyramid Style of News Reporting I

Reporters often use the inverted pyramid style as a way of assuring presentation of the most important news at the beginning of an article. This enables readers to quickly and easily grasp the sense of an article as well as the main facts.

1. What event will you write about? _____

   _____

2. What headline will you use to grab reader attention? _____

   _____

3. List the five Ws of the event in order of importance.

   _____

   _____

   _____

   _____

   _____

4. Note other interesting details in order of importance.

   _____

   _____

   _____

   _____

Name_____ Date_____

Inverted Pyramid Style of News Reporting II

Use the information on the reproducible on page 42 to write a brief article in the inverted pyramid. Place the headline in the top space.

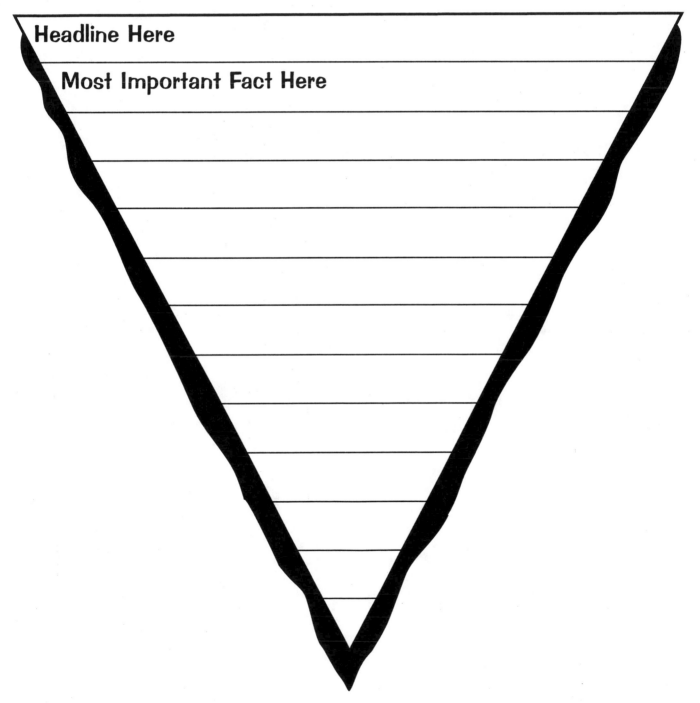

Headline Here

Most Important Fact Here

Editorial Style

Students use the editorial style when presenting opinions on timely issues, whether school related or of a more global nature. While it is still appropriate to include some or all of the five Ws, students are not limited to these facts when editorializing. They are now writing to persuade. Many students have strong opinions that are often based more on emotion than on reason. When writing editorials, it is important for students to understand that opinions must be supported by facts, and that a compelling argument is rarely based on emotions alone. If students are looking to change the way people think, which is usually the reason for an editorial, then they must present a mix of fact and reasoned opinions.

Teaching Ideas Teaching Ideas Teaching Ideas

 Discuss with students the difference between fact and opinion. Ask for their definitions of each and guide them to an understanding of the use of each in editorial writing. Reiterate that facts alone belong in straight news articles, while well-reasoned opinions (opinions supported by facts) belong in editorials. Provide articles and editorials from newspapers (both national, community, and school) and challenge students to find articles where reporters mix the two.

 Provide examples of editorials from local or national newspapers that deal with topics that students can relate to, such as funding for school sports or arts programs. Invite students to read the editorial. Conduct a follow-up discussion in which students express their own opinions on the issue as well as discussing the power of the editorial that was shared. Excellent editorials always inspire excellent discussion. Poll students to see if any minds were changed by the editorial. *It is important and valuable to provide as many real-life examples of excellent newspaper work as you can find*, whether from local and national newspapers or publications from other elementary and middle schools.

 Have students brainstorm possible editorial topics. Examples might include weekend homework, school uniforms, standardized testing, wearing hats in school, school-wide discipline methods, allowances, junk food in the cafeteria, dress codes, cell phones in school, "public display of affection," school dances, or backpacks in the classroom. Help students decide on one or two topics that everyone has strong feelings about. Be sure they understand that *it is important that editorials "speak" to a large number of people, no matter how those people feel about an issue.* Editorials on obscure topics that impact only a few people carry little weight. With limited space available, only editorials on topics of widespread interest will end up in print.

 Invite students to write editorials on the topic you have selected with input from the class. The reproducibles on pages 46-47 will help students organize their thoughts before writing and assess their work when it is complete. Students will state their opinions and provide at least three reasons in support of their opinion. You may wish to invite them to mention at least two reasons for the opposite view, particularly if those reasons can be successfully challenged or disproved by factual observations.

 Editorials provide an opportunity to practice writing interesting leads that are not purely statements of facts. While the situation inspiring the editorial should be stated clearly and succinctly, there is also room for thought-provoking comment. You may wish to have each student write an editorial lead for the same topic and share the leads for constructive criticism and discussion.

A Few More Ways to Say "Said"

Elaborated	★	Hesitated	★	Insisted
Emphasized		Hinted		Instructed
Exclaimed	★	Implied	★	Lamented
Explained		Indicated		Lectured
Fumed	★	Informed	★	Maintained
Grumbled		Inquired		Mentioned

Name _____ **Date** _____

Organizing an Editorial

Effective, compelling editorials are well-organized, succinct, and powerful. Organize your thoughts by answering the questions below.

1. What issue will you write about? _____

   _____

2. What headline will you use to draw attention to your editorial? _____

   _____

   _____

3. What is your opinion on the issue? _____

   _____

   _____

4. What are three reasons for your opinions? _____

   _____

   _____

   _____

5. What are two reasons why someone might disagree? _____

   _____

   _____

46

6. Write the lead for your editorial. _____

_____

_____

7. On a separate sheet of paper, write your editorial using the information you have organized on this worksheet. When you have completed the editorial, use the checklist below to edit your work.

❏ My opinion is clearly stated at least once.

❏ I have provided at least three reasons for my opinion.

❏ I have supported my reasons with facts when possible.

❏ I have demonstrated understanding of the opposing point of view.

❏ I have written an appropriate headline.

❏ I have signed my work.

And Even More Ways to Say "Said"

Mumbled	Pleaded	Scolded
Murmured	Proclaimed	Screamed
Muttered	Protested	Shouted
Nagged	Questioned	Teased
Notified	Quibbled	Uttered
Objected	Recounted	Verified
Offered	Replied	Whispered
Persuaded	Reported	

Editorial Cartooning

When reporters want to express their opinions on timely topics in written form, they write editorials. And when artists want to express opinions on timely topics, they often create editorial cartoons. Often the artist's opinion is expressed through satire or by gently poking fun in a good-natured way.

It is important that students choose cartoon subjects most readers can relate to. You and your students may wish to brainstorm a list of issues facing the school and community. Subjects of recent editorials might work as well. Stress that *issues* rather than *individuals* should bear the brunt of the humor. Editorial cartoons should never be derisive.

Teaching Ideas Teaching Ideas Teaching Ideas

 **S**hare with students some examples of newspapers or magazines that address issues that students can appreciate. Political cartoons are abundant. The Ellis Island immigration situation spawned hundreds of editorial cartoons that are readily available as well. Discuss the concept of satire (using humor, irony, or sarcasm to express a view) in both literature and in cartoon samples you have selected. Help students understand that cartoons must state opinions with simple illustrations and captions only.

 **P**ick a school issue that has been featured as a written editorial in your school newspaper or is slated for publication. Brainstorm ways to illustrate opinions on that issue. For example, perhaps students are not allowed to have soft drinks at school. You may have published student editorials on that issue, probably stating that students should be allowed that privilege. Lead students through the process of coming up with a cartoon to express their view of such a topic.

An example for the soft drink scenario might show students and teachers in the cafeteria. The students are drinking from clearly marked containers of milk, juice, or water. Over at the teachers' table, the faculty is hoisting clearly marked cans of soda. A word balloon emanating from one of the teachers says, "Not allowing students to have soft drinks is the best thing we've done!" Your newspaper staff will catch on quickly.

Invite students to choose topics from your list of ideas, choose positions, and draw cartoons. The best will end up in your newspaper.

Young C.J. joins the rest of the amateur athletes.

by Jack DePaolo

Editorial Cartooning Work Sheet

1. Name an issue on which you would like to express an opinion with an editorial cartoon. _____

   _____

2. What is your opinion on this issue? _____

   _____

   _____

   _____

3. List at least three reasons to support your opinion.

   1. _____

   2. _____

   3. _____

4. Draw a cartoon illustrating your position on this issue.

 50

Interviewing

The ability to conduct a good interview is a skill that will benefit students in a variety of areas. Every reporter on your staff should know how it's done. Your editors may choose to run a feature interview with a faculty member or student each month. Or interviews may simply provide quotes for regular news, sports, and feature articles. Either way, it is important that students observe some basic ground rules. Consider having them practice interviewing techniques with each other before going out on assignment. You may wish to use the reproducibles on pages 53-54 for this purpose. Share the following guidelines with students.

★ **M**ake an appointment well in advance of your interview. Introduce yourself, mention that you are a reporter for your school's newspaper, explain why you would like an interview, use *please* and *thank you*. Then, show up at least five minutes early.

Go to the interview prepared. Take your notebook and at least two pencils or pens. *Take a cassette recorder only if you have asked permission in advance.* If you're using a recorder, make sure it has fresh batteries, a good tape and a spare, and that you know how to use it. Make sure you take notes as a back-up. Wear your press badge.

Have at least fifteen questions prepared. Keep in mind the five Ws of news reporting. Avoid questions that require only *yes* or *no* answers.

List your questions in some kind of logical order. This will make more sense to your subject, and will make writing your story easier to organize and write. It is a good idea to leave space in your reporter's notebook for answers after each prepared question you've written down.

★ **B**e prepared for follow-up questions.

Ask your subject to spell any names you are unsure of.

Take careful notes. If you plan to quote your subject, make sure you have the quote word-for-word. Tape recorders come in handy here.

★ **O**ffer to bring the first or second draft to your subject for approval.

☆ **L**eave your newspaper business card with the person you are interviewing. Make sure you have his or her address and phone number for follow-up questions and so that you can send a copy of the published article. Thank your subject for his or her time before leaving.

Students may try to run the questions and answers word-for-word as their entire story. While on occasion this has its place, it is preferable and far more interesting to turn the questions and answers into a narrative and alternate between facts, quotes, and statements. For example, instead of writing *Q: When did you become interested in photography? A: When my uncle gave me a camera. I was about five years old*, a reporter could write, *Annie became interested in photography at age five, when her uncle gave her a camera.*

If reporters find out he or she doesn't have enough "good" material to write a good article, it's ususally because the questions weren't "good" enough. It's better to go to the interview with more instead of less prepared questions.

by Tucker Abbott

Name _____ **Date** _____ **Interviewee** _____

Interview Icebreaker

Who

has influenced you the most? _____

is your favorite teacher? _____
(Note: this question could lead to hurt feelings if asked of a current student about a current teacher.)

is your hero? _____

would you most like to meet? _____

What is your

favorite movie? _____

favorite book? _____

favorite TV show? _____

favorite subject in school? _____

favorite sport or hobby? _____

career choice? _____

pet peeve? _____

When

were you the happiest? _____

were you the saddest? _____

is your birthday? _____

Where

did you grow up? _____

would you like to visit? _____

did you spend your best vacation ever? _____

How

old are you? _____

would you describe yourself, using three adjectives? _____

would you spend your ideal day? _____

_____

_____

will you want to be remembered? _____

Why to any of the above questions _____

_____

_____

_____

_____

_____

54

Hosting a Press Conference

A press conference is a wonderful way to improve interviewing and news-writing skills. While a press conference is something your staff needs to prepare for, it is also terrific practice in "thinking on one's feet."

Start by inviting someone in the school, such as a new teacher, the principal, or a student in the news. As students improve their interviewing skills, you may decide to host a press conference with a member of the city council, a local journalist, or even the mayor. When you're ready for the big time, try a local published author, visiting dignitary, state-level politician, corporate executive, or president of a local college. And when you're ready to make news yourself, try to arrange for press conferences with performers, professional athletes, politicians on the federal level, and anyone else who you discover is coming to town.

Teach students that the best journalists are those who follow the news themselves. You'll have to get to work on the details of securing guests as soon as you hear of their impending arrival. The staff of *Carolina Kids' News*, my fifth graders, had the honor of hosting a press conference with Ben Cohen and Jerry Greenfield, founders of Ben & Jerry's Vermont Homemade, Inc.® ice cream. They also interviewed a three-time Pulitzer prize-winning cartoonist. These were certainly some of the highlights of these students' school years and definitely of their young journalist careers. Here are some tips for successful press conferences.

• ★ • ★ • ★ Prior to the Conference ★ • ★ • ★ •

Do your research and share it with students. Invite students to do some as well. Read biographies, corporate reports, press kits, news articles, and any other relevant materials.

Have each student write at least three interesting questions—questions that require more than a *yes* or *no* answer and that students cannot answer after having done the research.

Practice asking questions.

★ • ★ • ★ • During the Conference • ★ • ★ • ★

Ask students to wear press badges and have their notebooks, two pens or pencils, and their prepared questions.

Instruct students to listen carefully so they don't repeat a question.

Encourage students to state their names when called on to ask a question.

Tell them to wait patiently while answers are given and say thank you after their questions are answered.

Have them take good notes. If you have permission, tape the press conference as well.

• ★ • ★ • ★ After the Conference • ★ • ★ • ★

Be sure that the press conference leads to a newspaper article. This isn't *just* for practice. This way, students will understand the importance of taking good notes, listening to questions from others, and organizing their thoughts for the purpose of producing an article.

Teach the concept of story angles. A press conference can lead to several different articles—all in the same issue. What makes each article different is the approach or angle your reporters take. For example, the Ben and Jerry press conference led to stories on:

1. the actual press conference—questions and answers in article form

2. what it was like to be involved in a major press conference from a reporter's point of view

3. an article on the Ben & Jerry's Vermont Homemade, Inc. ® company

4. a feature story on what it took to bring Ben and Jerry to town

Other angles could have also been explored, such as a poll of favorite Ben & Jerry's ice cream flavors, a consumer-report style comparison of Ben & Jerry's ice cream to other brands, and a sidebar listing some of the many Ben & Jerry's charities.

★ • ★ • ★ After the Articles Are Published ★ • ★ • ★

Be sure a copy or two of your newspaper gets mailed to the people who came by for the press conference. Enclose a special thank-you note.

Proofreading and Editing

These symbols are the ones most commonly used in editing. Many others can be found in style books, writing manuals, and dictionaries. Encourage students to use these symbols whenever they do any editing or proofreading, and model their use yourself as often as possible.

∧	**Add something that is missing**	We can't make the meeting.
⊙	**Add a period**	Your work is due on Monday⊙
⌃	**Add a comma**	The cafeteria served hot dogs‚ fries, and milk.
∽	**Transpose**	Reveiw your assignments.
ℓ	**Delete**	Do your best always.
······	**Stet** (disregard edit symbol)	Do your best always.
═	**Use uppercase**	Our advisor, Mrs. davis, is out.
/	**Use lowercase**	Our Newspaper is the best!
¶	**Start a new paragraph**	¶Nothing can beat school news!
awk	**Awkward or confusing passage**	It happened tomorrow. awk
sp	**Check your spelling**	I can't reed your writing!
#	**Insert a space**	Give your article to me.
⌒	**Delete a space, close up**	Class room

Layout and Design

Your newspaper may not have professional layout artists and graphic designers on staff, but that is no reason for your newspaper to be anything less than terrific. There is no mystery to laying out an attractive, award-winning page. The rules are the same, whether you do paste-ups by hand or on the computer. The following guidelines will help.

1. Develop a style sheet for your newspaper (see page 22 for a sample). The style sheet should include all the rules you want your students to follow as they lay out each issue. Even if every page is designed by a different student, the newspaper will still have a cohesive look and feel if students follow your guidelines. The style sheet should address such issues as the following.

When and where to use quotes.

How to designate media titles
(capitalization, underline, quotation marks, italics, or a combination of these)

How to deal with numbers at the beginnings of sentences and in context
(numerals or words)

How to deal with the first and subsequent mentions of people's names

What point size and font to use for copy or text
(these should *never* vary)

What point size and font to use for bylines and captions
(these should *never* vary)

2. To keep your newspaper from taking on a ransom-note look, try to choose one font and have your students stick to it. Today's software provides a number of variations on fonts such as Times or Helvetica—bold, italics, outline, small caps—and it makes sound design sense to stick to one font. If you and your students are happier using two fonts, be consistent in how they are used. For example, all bylines should look identical, as should all text. However, a byline could be in Helvetica and text could be in Times if you wish to mix fonts. Good design often calls for using a serif font for body copy and a sans serif font for headlines.

3. Include at least one photo or graphic per page. Be sure they have captions. When your students lay out the paper, encourage them to look at spreads (two facing pages) and to place the graphics in different locations on each facing page. For example, you might place a photo in the upper left-hand corner of a left-hand page and another photo or a cartoon in the center of the right-hand column on the facing page. This provides more visual interest.

4. Help students strive for a balance of text, graphics, and white space on each page. A page crammed with text looks uninviting. A page with a lot of empty space looks poorly planned, as if something were missing. Keep a ready supply of editorial or noneditorial cartoons and article-related photos to use for filling extra space. If students are pasting up the paper by hand, be sure outside margins are absolutely consistent. These margins may be drawn on the pages they are pasting articles onto with a non-reproducible blue pencil (any light blue will work). Margins should be at least 1/2 inch (1.25 cm) around the outside and at least 3/8 inch (1 cm) between columns.

T.V. Turnoff was easy!

by Adam Schwartz

5. Include sidebars as a graphic feature. A sidebar is a small column, often shaded, boxed, or both, that includes accompanying information about some aspect of a feature article. For example, you might include where to write for more information, telephone numbers, facts that go along with an article, or a graph.

6. Decide or have students decide whether they prefer the newspaper columns to be justified (flush left and right) or flush left, ragged right. Justifying text in columns often creates bizarre word spacing and an inordinate number of hyphenated words which may appear unattractive to your staff. On the other hand, justified columns may appear to be neater. It's up to you and the students—but every page should follow the same format.

7. If students are pasting up the paper by hand, insist that every piece of text and every headline run exactly horizontal. Nothing makes a newspaper look more amateur than when some lines of text run uphill, some downhill, and headlines go every which way. A plastic T square makes this job simple. If you're unfamiliar with how to use a T square, an art teacher will be able to demonstrate. Of course, use of computer software solves this problem nicely. However, even with sophisticated software it's possible you're still pasting up small bits and pieces of the paper. Use that T square.

8. When laying out the paper, consider leaving 2 or 3 inches (5. to 7.5 cm) of column space on the front page for late-breaking news. This will give the paper a more timely feel. If nothing occurs that merits stopping the presses, substitute other short articles from your files. Keep a file of excellent articles that didn't make prior editions for just such a need, or consider using a photo or cartoon.

A Few Commonly Misspelled Words

Accessory	Cemetery	Forty
Achievement	Commitment	Government
A lot	Confident	Grammar
All right	Deceive	Gymnasium
Athletics	Embarrass	Inflammable
Bicycle	Encyclopedia	Kindergarten
Calendar	February	Library

Photography

The use of photographs add a whole new dimension to school newspaper. While clip art may be attractive and useful, nothing beats having a variety of student photographs in each issue. Students are absolutely capable of taking photographs that will work well and, like you, they will improve with practice. Here are some guidelines.

Camera Options ★ Camera Options ★ Camera Options

Digital

Digital is the way to go for most school photography if you can afford a decent camera. And the news is good. Digital cameras continue to drop in price. You will likely pay for your camera in saved film and processing costs and halftone creation in just a couple of years at most. And with digital, your students (or you) can tell right that minute if the shot "worked." Otherwise, take another one, or another, or another. You should get a digital with at least 3 or 4 mega-pixel resolution capability. While virtually none of your photos will be printed as 8 X 10s in your newspaper, it's nice to have the extra resolution so that you have extra quality for printing. Make sure you know how to set the various "qualities" or resolutions on your camera. What looks great on your computer monitor might only print marginally in your paper. Printers like photos with a resolution of at least 300 dpi (dots per inch) equivalency. Many digitals will be pre-set at only 72 dpi, which is all you need for emailing and for viewing online. So, get out the manual and change that setting. A good optical zoom is important and will provide much more clarity than a digital zoom. Cameras with easy to find and understand control buttons and dials will make life easier.

You will need to decide how you're getting your digitals from the camera into the computer. While all digitals store their images on memory cards of some type, it might be laborious to have only one computer hooked up with a card reader or the software to download the images. An option is a digital that uses a standard floppy and will fit into any computer. Those cameras tend to be larger and the floppy does not store as many images as the smaller memory cards. While this will probably not be an issue for most staffs—it's worth considering.

Film Camera

Certainly, it's not time to throw away that good 35mm camera. A good quality point-and-shoot automatic 35mm camera will get you just the shot you need. Auto-focus is standard on most of these cameras and is worth having. You will also want a built-in flash. A film auto-loading feature would be another excellent plus. Loading film improperly seems to rank up there with not setting correct film speed as a major problem on photo assignments. Just about all of these problems are handled by today's cameras. Most processing companies won't charge you for a blank roll of film, but your photo op may be long gone.

Getting the Images on the Page

Not really a problem. With digital it's a snap because the image is already "digitized" and ready for placement. With an actual paper photograph, it will need to be scanned. Make sure you scan the photo at 300 dpi. With both processes (digital and scanning), you should convert the photograph to gray scale, crop it, fix the brightness and contrast, and take care of other small "mistakes" before inserting the photo. If you are using a film camera and don't have a scanner, you will need to have your printer create a halftone for each photo. This is the process of converting the image to a series of little dots (that's those dots per inch I was talking about). There will be a charge for this, and you'll quickly see where digital will pay for itself in no time at all.

Photography Hints for Students

Be sure you know how to load and use the camera. If you are not sure, ask for a demonstration. If necessary, set the film speed. (The ISO number is listed on the film box and on the film itself.) Some cameras, usually labeled DX, will set the speed automatically—check the manual for details. Even digital cameras need to have their "film speed or ISO equivalency" changed to a higher number if you're attempting to get clear action shots. Never go off on assignment without practice. Here are some tips.

Hold the camera steady or you'll end up with a blurry photo.

Troubleshooting Hint: If you get your pictures back and everything is blurry, chances are you moved the camera while pressing the shutter release button. If only the subject is blurry, the subject probably moved or you didn't have the subject in focus. Use a monopod as a means of holding the camera steady. By the way, if you end up with an out-of-focus photo; don't use it in your paper.

Squeeze the shutter release with slow, even pressure.

Troubleshooting Hint: Take a big breath, let out half, then very gently press the shutter release.

Get up close.

Troubleshooting Hint: Most 35mm cameras, even the fixed-focus types, and digitals will take a good photo at four feet (1.2 meters). Photograph people at about this range. Read the instruction manual to determine the exact close-focusing point.

Keep the background simple.

Troubleshooting Hint: Put your eye as close to the viewfinder as possible when framing a photo. Then, look carefully at what's behind your subject. This will prevent you from ending up with a photo that shows a branch growing out of your subject's ear. Avoid taking photos when directly facing glass such as a window or trophy case. The flash will reflect back, producing a huge glaring hot spot on your final photo. If you must take a picture with glass behind or as the subject, take the picture at a 45-degree angle to the reflective surface.

Use the flash.

Troubleshooting Hint: Flash should always be used indoors and often outdoors to lighten shadows on your subject's face. Be sure you know how to operate the flash—even automatic cameras may require flash activation. Digitals often have the capability of making the most of available light, but the flash is still often needed to lighten shadows or add contrast to your photographs.

Take notes.

Troubleshooting Hint: Have your notebook handy. It's when you take the picture that you get information for the caption, including full names of people; the order in which they appear, such as left to right; and other important information. It's a good idea to get a contact's phone number in case you have to call for additional information. Keep that number in your reporter's notebook.

In most cases, take pictures of people at eye level.

Troubleshooting Hint: If you're trying to make some sort of photographic statement, you might experiment with pictures taken from different levels. Shooting a person from above makes the person appear smaller. Similarly, shooting from a low angle makes the person appear larger. Do try some variety in your shots though. It will get boring if every single photograph in your newspaper is taken straight on with the subject in the center.

Take more than one photo of each scene.

Troubleshooting Hint: Pros learn early to bracket exposure, which means taking one picture at the normal light setting, one slightly underexposed, and the other slightly overexposed. If your camera is automatic, you may not be able to try this technique. However, always take a second or third shot of each scene. This helps guarantee at least one perfectly exposed, clear shot. With a digital, this will cost you nothing but a little extra time. And with digital, you'll know right then and there if a photo will "work" for your purposes. Even so, take more than one photo.

Sports photography is a challenge.

There are several techniques to help catch the action and make it dramatic at the same time. One is to look for "peak action" of the activity. For example, if you wait until the instant the basketball player is at the peak of a jump, there will be a brief instant before he or she falls back to earth. That's when to snap the picture. Almost all fast sports include this brief instant at peak action; a hurdler at the top of a hurdle or a tennis player poised to slam a serve are good examples.

Troubleshooting Hint: always using the fastest (highest number) film speed available—400 and 800 ISO film is good. You might find that the 800 film is a little on the grainy side, but this might be what you have to have for indoor sports photography. Even digital cameras should be set to a higher "film speed" setting. And use flash when taking sports photos indoors, even if your camera says you don't need it. The burst of flash will help stop the action. Get as close to the action as possible. If you are farther than 20 feet away, your photo may be disappointing. It's wise to use a monopod for all sports photography, indoors or out. And some sports photographers find that they get the best shots by setting up in one specific spot courtside or fieldside and waiting for the action to come into their range. Others prefer to walk up and down looking for the best shot.

Composition—arranging the subject and other elements in the viewfinder in a pleasing fashion—is important. Sports photos are hard enough to capture without thinking about composition. But if you can, and your photo is part of a photo essay or feature, take the time to compose your picture.

Troubleshooting Hint: To give your photos more life and impact, try shooting from different angles. Also, use the "rule of thirds," which says that you should try to place your main subject off-center as opposed to directly in the center of the viewfinder. Imagine that your viewfinder is divided into thirds by vertical and horizontal lines. Try to put your main subject where two of the lines intersect (see diagram). If you have two subjects, try to put one subject at one intersecting point (for example, top left) and the other main subject at the opposite intersecting point (bottom right). Normally, the subject should look into the photo, not into the border.

The Rule of Thirds

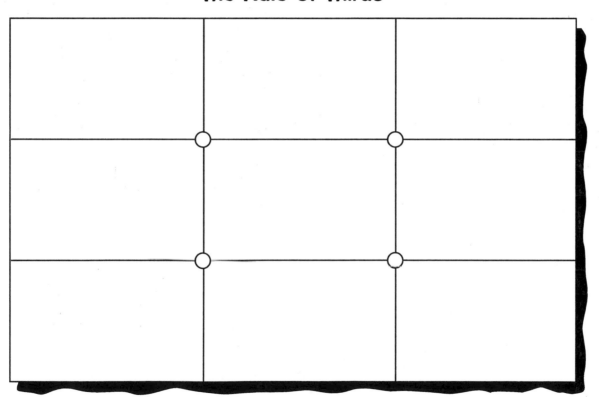

Generating the Newspaper

There are many ways of publishing your final product, and school newspapers seem to run the gamut. While each method may have advantages and disadvantages, desktop publishing is the hands-down favorite.

What follows represents a progression of publishing possibilities. Start wherever you feel most comfortable. Don't be surprised if your students are higher on the scale than you are!

1. Use hammer, chisel, and stone to record the news. Slow, but absolutely permanent. However, it's not very practical.

2. Use a manual typewriter (if you can still find one) and type directly onto what will be your camera-ready pages. Definitely faster than Number 1. A student or teacher does the typing. Replacing the manual with an electric one speeds up the process somewhat.

3. Use the old noncomputer cut-and-paste method—you or your students type individual articles using a typewriter or word processor and paste them onto layout pages within light blue-ruled margins (your proofs) for photocopying. This method is used by quite a few schools, though those numbers are dwindling. If you paste or photocopy onto 11 inches X 17 inches (27.5 cm X 42.5 cm) paper, you create a newspaper that may be folded rather than stapled. This process introduces some interesting pagination exercises and also requires that the paper have an even number of pages. There can always be a loose 8 1/2 inches X 11 inches (20 cm X 27.5 cm) insert so that the total page count need not be a multiple of four.

4. Use the computer-generated cut-and-paste method, where students input their individual articles on computers and you or an editor use the cut-and-paste feature of your computer software to arrange the articles on final pages ready for print-out and reproduction. This method is used by most schools. Ideally, the entire process is done by students with the teacher remaining in an advisory capacity. Students save their articles on disks, and editors create the layout by importing each article into the final document. If your school is wired to a central server, it is far preferable to save individual articles there. Then, you don't have to worry about an individual student's disk failing. Plus, you have the added benefit of being able to pull up a particular article or page from any computer on the system. The entire staff helps proof, edit, and revise before the paper is printed. There are plenty of publishing programs available from those primarily intended for younger students to those meant for layout professionals. And with practice, your students will be mastering whatever software you use. Microsoft Publisher is a popular program that students quickly learn. Adobe's PageMaker and InDesign are examples of full-featured programs.

Funding the Newspaper

Raising the funds to support your newspaper may or may not be a challenge, depending on your school's finances. You and your student business manager should begin by preparing a budget, using the work sheet on page 69. The least expensive newspapers are photocopied right on the school copier with no expense billed to the classroom. The most expensive are sent out for professional printing, folding, and collating. Assuming all school papers will need some funding, here are some possibilities.

★ **T**ry for full or partial funding in the school budget. Use the justifiable argument that publishing a newspaper will be an important part of your language arts program, and students will learn real-life skills, and will produce a wonderful public-relations tool for the school. And wow, what a writing program you'll have!

★ **S**ell subscriptions. Many school like to distribute their newspapers for free, but some sell yearly subscriptions or individual copies.

★ **S**ell copies from a newspaper box at a neighborhood store or in your school lobby. Some city newspapers might be willing to donate a used coin-operated paper box for your use. Paint the box and print new signs using your laser printer. Your students will take pride in seeing their paper being made available to the general public. They'll take even more pride when they see a *stranger* buying a copy.

★ **S**ell subscriptions to students' grandparents, uncles and aunts, and distant friends. Mail these out by first class mail. Grandparents will love seeing the work of their grandchildren. Often, parents will sign up the grandparents and pay for the subscriptions themselves.

★ **S**ell advertisements. This can be a large source of income, but it can also take up a great deal of space. It also takes up a great deal of time. The ads will have to be designed and space reserved. You'll need to make sure a paid advertisement doesn't get left out.

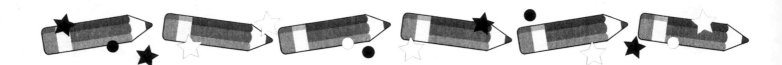

★ **S**ell underwriting. Instead of ads, ask parents and businesses to be underwriters. List their names in a box in each issue stating that the newspaper is supported in part (or in whole) by the following friends and businesses.

★ **A**pply for grants. They take time to write but could provide complete funding for your paper. Certainly, plenty of other people will see the value of using a student newspaper as a means of improving writing and other language arts skills.

★ **H**old bake sales and the other usual fund-raising events. Enlist the help of PTA members. They are usually fund-raising experts and may be willing to help fund the newspaper.

★ **I**nvite underwriting by a local newspaper or print shop—or ask to be a business "partner" with that newspaper or print shop. If you are extraordinarily fortunate, you may find that your local newspaper or printing company will print your paper for free. It's great publicity for them. If they aren't willing to print at no charge, they may do the work at a fraction of the usual cost. Just ask. Make sure you include a notice in your paper showing your appreciation for their support.

A Few Commonly Misspelled Words

Maintenance	Receive	Their
Mathematics	Restaurant	Tomorrow
Occasion	Scholastic	Twelfth
Pamphlet	Scissors	Wednesday
Parallel	Separate	Weight
Physician	Superintendent	Weird
Poison		

Budget Work Sheet

Use this work sheet to estimate the funding needed to publish your newspaper. Estimate the number of issues you wish to publish and multiply the total production and distribution costs by that number. Add this to total start-up expenses to reach your grand total. Hopefully, you will find the major purchase items already at hand in your classroom or school computer lab.

Start-up Costs
Software (clip art, desktop-publishing program) $ _____
Hardware (computer, printer, scanner) $ _____
Office Supplies $ _____
Other Purchases (camera, film, etc.) $ _____
  Total Start-up (1) $ _____

Production Costs (per issue)
Photography (film, developing) $ _____
Halftone conversion (if necessary) $ _____
Printing, folding, collating $ _____
  Total Production (2) $ _____

Distribution Costs (per issue)
Postage and envelopes for mailing newspaper (3) $ _____

  Total Production + Distribution (2) + (3) $ _____

  Total Cost per Issue (2) + (3)
  X Number of Issues to be Published $ _____

  + Total Start-up (1) $ _____

  Grand Total $ _____

Other Publishing Ideas

Publishing a newspaper is time-consuming. But once you and your students get the hang of it, it will (almost) run itself. As you develop systems for handling the details, you will find that students are able to do more and more of the work themselves. So if you've found that you have a little time to spare and the kids are chomping at the bit to write and publish, you may wish to consider some of the following.

• ★ • ★ • Desktop Publishing Company • ★ • ★ •

Form a publishing company and give it a name. Like the newspaper, this becomes a business run by students. Create a marketing team to get the word out to teachers and other staff members that you're in business and can provide useful services at no charge. Sometimes the customer may wish to provide special paper.

Obtain software such as *Print Shop* from Broderbund or Microsoft's *Publisher* or any of the inexpensive layout programs you can find at a large office supply store. Add a CD collection of tens of thousands of pieces of clipart and a laser printer, and your students can create professional-quality name labels, letterhead, thank-you notes, name badges, business cards, grading rubrics, membership cards, flyers, admission tickets, and dozens of other things. Try to avoid any business that involves a tremendous amount of text—it is hard for kids to proofread everything. These services are appreciated by the teachers, and the work is visible throughout the school. Often you'll find two or three students who are accomplished enough to serve as the instructors.

★ • ★ • ★ Student Yellow Pages ★ • ★ • ★

A handy reference, the Student Yellow Pages, is published once or twice a year and contains services that students themselves can offer. Invite your newspaper staff to develop a form to distribute to the entire student body. Provide a place on the form for parent signatures before accepting "advertising" in your Yellow Pages. Like the real Yellow Pages, you can list categories such as card-collection traders, tutors, computer wizards, pet sitters, and so on. Students fill out the forms, return them to your staff, and then the staff publishes the newest edition of your school's Yellow Pages.

70

• ★ • ★ • Class Newsletters • ★ • ★ •

There is nothing new about class newsletters that go home every week or two. Many teachers fret over this type of good communication tool each time they sit down at the keyboard. Well, fret no more. Assign two or three students to be class newsletter editors for each issue. Set a deadline, explain what you want included in each issue, and leave the rest up to them. It will become a contest of sorts to see which group of editors can come up with the best newsletter. Keep the same title each week. You may want to design the masthead or nameplate yourself so that students need only write, edit, and lay out the articles. Not only will they get extra practice in writing, layout design, and editing, but your students' parents will appreciate the home-school communication. And of course, you'll have one less job to do each week.

★ • ★ Special Issues of the Newspaper ★ • ★

If you can't manage enough times for regular issues of a school newspaper, try a special edition newspaper once or twice a year. Possibilities include the following.

1. *Moving Up* issue: For example, a middle school sixth grade class could write and publish a special newspaper for incoming fifth graders.

2. *Welcome to Our School* issue: This is a wonderful public-relations tool written by your students. This special publication would include everything a new student, teacher, family moving to town, or school visitor would want to know about the school. Your school's office and the district office love to have copies as well as local real estate agents.

3. *Newspaper of the Future*: Print creative articles on what students think school will be like in the future. Pick a date—any date—for reference, and let them take off. It will be an interesting issue to write, fun to read, and perfect to place in a time capsule for future reference.

Real-World Publishing Opportunities for Kids—Projects for Your Classroom Publishing Center offers dozens of other suggestions. See resources on page 79 for information.

Assessment Sheet — Copy

Issue Date _____ Page Number _____

Article Headline _____

Staff member(s) responsible for this article _____

_____

_____

_____

✔+ Excellent   ✔Good   ✔- Not meeting standards

_____ Headline (good choice of words)   ★ _____ Spelling

_____ Lead sentence sets the tone.   ★ _____ Punctuation

_____ Article answers five Ws.   _____ Article follows style sheet.

_____ Article contains accurate information.   ★ _____

_____ Article has good closing.   ★ _____

Final Grade _____

Notes _____

_____

_____

_____

_____

 72

Assessment Sheet — Page Layout

Issue Date _____ **Page Number** _____

Article Headline _____

Staff member(s) responsible for this article _____

_____

_____

_____

✔+ **Excellent**   ✔ **Good**   ✔- **Not meeting standards**

_____ Headlines are boldface and centered.

_____ Byline is centered and not boldface.

_____ Page includes at least one graphic.

_____ Graphics are appropriate.

_____ Captions are included for photos and graphics.

_____ Overall layout is neat and attractive.

_____ Page number is in proper place.

_____ Margins meet guidelines.

_____

_____

_____

Final Grade _____

Notes _____

_____

_____

_____

Assessment Sheet —Copy and Layout

Issue Date _____ Page Number _____

Article Headline _____

Staff member(s) responsible for this article _____

_____

_____

_____

✔+ Excellent   ✔Good   ✔- Not meeting standards

_____ Headline (good choice of words)

_____ Lead sentence sets the tone.

_____ Article answers five Ws.

_____ Article contains accurate information.

_____ Article has a good closing.

_____ Spelling

_____ Punctuation

_____ Article follows a style sheet.

_____ Headlines are boldface and centered; byline is not boldface.

_____ Page includes at least one graphic; captions are used for graphics.

_____ Design of page is pleasing (proper margins, page number in correct location, white space is appropriate).

| Final Grade _____ |

Notes _____

_____

_____

_____

Organizations

National Elementary Schools Press Association (NESPA)
Carolina Day School
1345 Hendersonville Road
Asheville, NC 28803
828/ 274-0758 X385
info@nespa.org
www.nespa.org

NESPA offers help for elementary and middle schools that publish or are planning to publish a school or class newspaper. NESPA publishes an online newsletter (*Nespaper*), provides a site for students to publish their work in syndication, offers a newspaper rating and review service, and helps facilitate sharing of school newspapers through "NewsShare."

Journalism Education Association (JEA)
Kansas State University
103 Kedzie Hall
Manhattan, KS 66506-1505
785/ 532-5532
www.jea.org

JEA offers help primarily for high schools and middle schools. Publishes a newsletter online, membership directory and a quarterly journal, *Communication: Journalism Education Today.* Has a well-supplied catalog filled with books on all aspects of publishing including newspapers, magazines, and yearbooks. Plenty of how-to information for desktop publishing. JEA and National Scholastic Press Association hold a combined national high school journalism convention each year in both fall and spring. Many sessions are geared especially toward middle school students and advisors.

National Scholastic Press Association (NSPA)
2221 University Avenue, SE
Suite 121
Minneapolis, MN 55414
612/ 625-8335
www.studentpress.org/nspa

NSPA offers help primarily for high schools. Sponsors a national judging service for school newspapers and yearbooks. Co-sponsors with JEA a national high school journalism convention twice a year at various locations around the country.

Quill and Scroll Society
School of Journalism and Mass Communication
University of Iowa
Iowa City, IA 52242-1528
319/ 335-5795
www.uiowa.edu/~quill-sc

The Quill and Scroll Society charters schools as members and serves as an honorary society for scholastic journalists.

Newspaper in Education (NIE)
NIE works through the local city newspaper and schools by providing teaching materials to go along with regular deliveries of city newspapers. While their primary focus is to help teachers use the local newspaper as a teaching tool, schools can learn all about newspapers through the service. Each NIE city newspaper has a NIE Manager-School Coordinator who can arrange tours of the newspaper plant and editorial and publication offices as well as provide other learning materials. Contact your local paper to see if they are a NIE member newspaper.

Student Press Law Center (SPLC)
1101 Wilson Blvd., Suite 1100
Arlington, VA 22209-2211
703/ 807-1904
www.splc.org

The Student Press Law Center offers free help and information on media law topics. Call them when you think you need legal help, or better yet, for help on how to stay out of trouble.

The Poynter Institute
801 Third Street South
St. Petersburg, FL 33701
888/ 769-6837
www.poynter.org

The Poynter Institute provides news articles, commentary, seminars, information, a high school journalism guide, and "everything you need to be a better journalist." The information is mostly for teachers, but student journalists interested in improving their craft would benefit.

American Society of Newspaper Editors
11690B Sunrise Valley Drive
Reston, VA 20191
703/ 453-1122
www.asne.org

ASNE is included here because of a really wonderful program they have for elementary, middle, and high schools. For a very small fee, they offer the software and templates for you and your students to publish an online edition of your newspaper. Elementary and middle schools should check out the information at: my.schooljournalism.org. High schools should go to: my.highschooljournalism.org. It's a bargain, but it gets even better. They throw in several free resource books when you sign up.

Newspaper Association of America Foundation (NAA)
1921 Gallows Road, Suite 600
Vienna, VA 22182-3900
703/ 902-1600
www.naa.org/foundation

NAA Foundation offers seed money grants each year to help establish or revive student newspapers. Funds can be used for production and distribution costs and to train the adviser and staff members.

Mind-Stretch Publishing
3124 Landrum Road
Columbus, NC 28722
828/ 863-4235
www.mindstretch.com

The publisher of this book and several other journalism resource books including *The Reporter's Notebook—Writing Tools for Student Journalists*. Mind-Stretch offers workshops for teachers and students on a variety of writing topics.

Catalogs of Journalism Books

JEA Catalog
(See address under organizations on page 75.)

Journalism Catalog
The Writing Company
800-421-4246
www.writingco.com

Books

These books are widely circulated and are usually easy to find in bookstores, directly from the publisher, or online through mass distributors such as Amazon.com and Barnes & Noble.

Associated Press (AP) Stylebook
AP Newsfeatures

The bible for professional newspaper editors nationwide—offers much for elementary and middle-school newspaper advisors as well. Contains definitive answers to just about any grammar, punctuation, capitalization, forms of address questions you might have.

EXp3 Journalism: A Handbook for Journalists
by Mark Levin
McGraw-Hill/Glencoe

A journalism textbook written with middle school students (and teachers) in mind. There is also a student workbook and a teacher's guide available.

Grant Writing for Teachers
by Linda Karges-Bone
School Specialty Children's Publishing

An easy-to-understand primer in writing grant proposals. Goes through the entire process from idea to budgeting. Sample work sheets included.

The Reporter's Notebook—Writing Tools for Student Journalists
by Mark Levin
Mind-Stretch Publishing

This handy reporter's notebook includes its own crash course in journalism, lots of organizational pages to keep your young reporters headed in the right direction, and plenty of note-taking pages spiced up with advice from professional writers and journalists.

Publishing With Students—A Comprehensive Guide
by Chris Weber
Heinemann Publishers

A collection of essays by inspired and inspiring writing teachers around the world who have helped students publish. The author has amassed an impressive collection of student samples that show you what is possible.

Real-World Publishing for Kids—Projects for Your Classroom Publishing Center
by Mark Lcvin
School Specialty Children's Publishing

Dozens of ideas of what your kids can publish beyond the newspaper. Some of the projects take an hour and others all year with most somewhere in-between. The book contains plenty of how-to help, organizational forms, project variations, and great ideas.

Other Resources

There is plenty of publishing software available today from office supply stores as well as educational software catalogs. Teachers can usually get the best deals through companies that deal with schools as their main business.

Catalogs to write for:

Educational Resources
P. O. Box 1900
Elgin, IL 60121-1900
800-624-2926
www.edresources.com

Specialty Software

Crossword Creator is an easy-to-use software program for creating word searches, crossword puzzles, and more.
Centron Software
800-848-2424
www.centronsoftware.com

Avery, the makers of hundreds of types of printer-ready labels and card stock, provides free templates online—perfect for making those press passes using blank business-card stock.
www.avery.com

Specialty Papers

Most school newspapers are printed on standard-sized copy paper. However, the following companies offer paper designed especially for newsletters that add real pizzazz to your product. In addition, there are papers for hundreds of other uses. Write for their free catalogs and samples.

Paper Direct
800-272-7377
www.paperdirect.com

Baudville
800-728-0888
www.baudville.com

Idea Art
800-433-2278
www.ideaart.com